THE UGLY TRUTH ABOUT

MEN!

A GUIDE TO THE WEAKER SEX

Written and Illustrated

By

Tom Carey

CCC Publications • Los Angeles

Published by

CCC Publications
21630 Lassen St.
Chatsworth, CA 91311

Copyright © 1992 Tom Carey

Manufactured in the United States Of America

Cover © 1992 CCC Publications

Interior Illustrations © 1992 Tom Carey & CCC Publications

Cover art by Don Vernon

Interior art by Tom Carey

Cover/Interior layout & production by Tim Bean/
DMC Publishing Group

ISBN: 0-918259-46-0

Pre-publication Edition - 9/92
First printing - 4/93

If your local U.S. bookstore is out of stock, copies of this book
may be obtained by mailing check or money order for $5.95 per
book (plus $2.50 to cover postage and handling) to:
CCC Publications; 21630 Lassen St. Chatsworth, CA 91311.

This book is dedicated
to all the good men I know.
Men whose exploits, foibles
and flaws made it possible.

And necessary.

But mostly,
it's for the women
who put up with all of us.

TABLE OF CONTENTS

INTRODUCTION

There are things that are puzzling about men.
There are questions that beg to be answered.
Mysteries that must be unravelled.
For instance:

1.) Why do men think that it's perfectly okay to clip their toenails over the coffee table?

2.) Why do they call their oldest and dearest pals by nick-names like "Ol' Butt Sniff?"

3.) Why do they think it's unmanly to cry and yet feel completely at ease hugging and rolling around in the mud together and patting each other on the rump?

4.) Do all men find the Three Stooges hilarious?

5.) Must they be completely fixated on the size of a woman's breasts?

6.) Why is it that, unless they're gay, they can't dress themselves without help?

7.) Do they think that plaid is a primary color or something?

8.) How can a man watch four college football games in a row on Saturday afternoon and then come back for more on Sunday?

9.) And then watch golf tournaments, too?

10.) Why is it that they are able to completely dismantle and reassemble an automobile engine but find it impossible to operate a vacuum cleaner?

11.) And **WHY OH WHY** don't they ever call when they say they will?

These are all **good** questions. These are all important questions. These are all questions that women have puzzled over through the ages.

And here are the answers:

1.) Because it keeps them from falling on the carpeting.
2.) Because of an incident that occurred in junior high school that's rather embarrassing.
3.) Just because it is.
4.) Yes.
5.) Yes.
6.) Who are you calling queer?
7.) Isn't it?
8.) Because football is a metaphor of life and it's fun to watch guys get their heads bashed in.
9.) Because you've got to have *something* to watch to kill time until dinner.
10.) Jeez, vacuum cleaners are complicated.
11.) What the hell was I *supposed* to say? Sorry, I had a miserable time and I never want to see you again?

Want more answers to *more* questions? Of course you do! You're a woman, and, by nature, a glutton for just exactly this sort of punishment.

Read on, then, and learn *The Ugly Truth About Men.*

Section One

HIS BODY, HIS SMELLS
The Ugly Truth About Jock Itch

Q. What exactly is "The Ugly Truth About Men?"

A. The ugly truth about men is that they snore. They snore, they have icy cold feet, they call out old girlfriend's names during sex and they can't begin to dress themselves without assistance from someone who isn't colorblind or totally devoid of a sense of style or taste. But, heck, you still love the cute little buggers anyway, don't you? Well? Don't you?

Q. Are men born brain damaged, or does some terrible, debilitating substance seep into their systems during childhood?

A. Nobody knows. Scientists and behaviorists battle endlessly over the question of which has more effect on human beings, genetics or environment. All we can know for sure about the male of the species is that he begins life in the womb almost indistinguishable from the female and somehow turns into a child who enjoys frying insects on the sidewalk with a magnifying glass and later develops into an adult who attends wrestling matches and picks his nose whenever he gets behind the wheel of a car.

It's a mystery all right. Are males born more aggressive than females or are they taught to be that way? There is plenty of evidence that points to dear old Dad as the culprit. Some researchers suggest that if boys were separated from their fathers at an early enough age they could be taught not to yell "Ooh Pah!" in crowded restaurants, not to douse their scrambled eggs in ketchup and not to refer to some areas of the female anatomy as "bodacious ta-tas."

Unfortunately, government research money needed for the continued study of these phenomena is a bit tough to come by due to the fact that most United States legislators are men who do all of these things.

Q. I swear if I weren't around to fix a decent meal once in a while, my fiance would die of malnutrition or rickets or something. Don't men care about their health enough to eat properly?

A. Most of the great chefs in the world are men, as any man will tell you if you get into an argument with him about which is really the weaker sex. What this has to do with anything at all is beyond me, but count on a man to use this argument when he feels the advantage slipping away.

Men don't eat well simply because they value their time too highly. Why should a man who scarfs up dinner in four minutes spend the better part of an hour cooking it?

Men like simple foods. By simple I mean that the packages are easy to open. Taste and ease of preparation are also high on the list of things men consider when choosing nourishment. Most men don't know quite where their food comes from. They think that hamburgers are just an unusual kind of vegetable that happen to grow in a paper wrapper with cheese melted on them. It is preferable to be with this kind of man, however, than with the other kind. The "other kind" is a man who has become so fanatical about food that he has to shop at special stores that use only natural fertilizers, takes four dozen vitamins twice a day, and goes into long heart-rending tales of dead baby cows when you order veal parmigiana in your favorite Italian restaraunt.

Q. My husband keeps me awake all night with the most godawful snoring I've ever heard. Short of sleeping in another state, what can I do?

A. As I said, men snore. They just do, and there's no way for *you* to stop them. There's also no way for you to convince them that they snore. "I didn't hear anything," he'll say, when you complain about averaging 35 minutes of sleep a night. This is an interesting argument considering that most men could doze quite comfortably in the percussion section of the London Philharmonic Orchestra during "The 1812 Overture."

Some women find that they can stop these broken buzz saw noises, at least temporarily, by nudging their snoozing mate or pushing him a little. Just moving his arm gently should do the trick. As long as you move it gently into his mouth.

THE FOUR MAJOR
MALE FOOD GROUPS

CANNED

FROZEN

TAKE OUT

DELIVERED

Q. Why is it that my husband refuses to admit it when he's lost? It always takes us twice as long as it should to get anywhere because we end up spending hours driving around in circles with him saying "We're not lost, it's got to be around here somewhere!"

A. Men are born adventurers. Deep in the soul of every man is the desire to roam the world at the helm of a great ship, to discover new and uncharted lands. Unfortunately, there's no such thing as uncharted land anymore (unless you count that Haitian "beachfront resort" property he bought as an "investment" five years ago), so for adventure your husband has to make do with finding your Aunt Hilda's Christmas party without using the directions she gave you.

Men love maps. Most men keep at least a couple dozen in the glove box of their car in case of emergency, although what good a map of "The Cowboy Museums of The Great Southwest" would be when you live in downtown Philadelphia is hard to say.

Men pride themselves on being great navigators and fearless drivers. Your husband would probably try to find Aunt Hilda's using a compass and sextant and plot out a course based on latitude and longitude if he thought you'd sit still for it.

The thought that a gas station attendant might know how to get somewhere better than him is unthinkable. Even if your husband is from Pleasantville, New Jersey, the gas station is in Paris, and he's been circling the city for three days in search of the Eiffel Tower.

Q. Why do men feel that it's necessary to pee everywhere? I'm sure that being able to go while standing is delightful, but why must they demonstrate it constantly?

A. Men are, by and large (or shall I say, small and large?), tremendously attached to their penises. And vice versa. A young man discovers at an early age the thrill of standing before the gleaming white porcelain of the public urinal with his own private little laser beam at hand, aiming at cigarette butts and gum wrappers and muttering "Zap! Blam! Ka-Pow! Die, alien invaders!" This is a pleasure a woman can never know, unless she develops incredible muscle control and the ability to hover. Men are glad to be as lavishly equipped as they are and often more than a little smug about it.

Men are tremendously territorial creatures and, just like the neighborhood dogs, they like to pee on their property to stake out territory. And while you may scoff at this, you'd be surprised how infrequently your neighbor asks to borrow your lawn mower once it's been peed upon. Well, maybe you wouldn't.

TEN FUN THINGS TO DO WHILE PEEING STANDING UP

1. Fill the bowl with foam.

2. Flush before you start and try to time it right to the finish.

3. Wash down the entire bowl and/or urinal.

4. Sword fight with a friend.

5. Try for distance records.

6. Aim at cigarette butts and gum wrappers.

7. Drill a hole in the urinal cake.

8. Write name in the snow.

9. Check out the size of the guy next to you.

10. Jiggle it.

___

Q. I swear my boyfriend's refrigerator is growing new life forms, and his shower curtain has just about hardened. It smells like a locker room, too. I can barely stand to go over there, but it doesn't seem to bother him a bit. What gives?

A. Clearly, men do not value cleanliness as much as women do. Or at all really. Although they will usually keep their automobiles and their golf clubs spotless. Does this necessarily make them worse human beings than women? Well, yes, probably.

A man's very idea of what is clean and what isn't is far different from a woman's and it has always been so. A lot of men see cleaning as a complete waste of energy. Why make the bed, a man thinks, when I'm just going to get back in it and mess it up again tonight? Why shovel the snow? It'll melt someday. Indeed, why clean at all, he'll think, I'll be dead eventually and where will all that extra work have gotten me?

A man takes cleaning action only as a desperate last resort. Like when empty beer cans and pretzel bags have piled up so high that they block the TV, or when the shower drain gets so backed up that his shins get high water marks.

Man's disdain for cleanliness originated way back in pre-historic times. Back in those days, smelling like his surroundings was a desirable trait in a man because it allowed him to sneak up behind his animal adversaries and whack them with a club.

Sure, most Neanderthal dudes were forgetful about birthdays and anniversaries and lousy at oral sex. And most weren't much for little romantic gestures, like leaving love notes on the cave walls where a cave woman could be surprised by them, but they did make up for such short-comings by being fearless (and fragrant) hunters and excellent providers. Plus, there was a good chance that a cave man who blended in well with his environment would survive awhile, no mean feat in an era of twelve-year life expectancies.

Unfortunately for today's women, men are fighting a losing battle against thousands of years of genetic coding. The male gene pool is swimming with grunge-loving chromosomes. It's no longer survival of the smelliest, but I'm afraid many men still feel the effects of their ancestry. They still smell bad and they're still lousy at oral sex.

Q. What goes on in the bathroom that is so entrancing that he has to sit in there for hours at a time? I mean, what the heck is he doing in there?

A. A man's bathroom is his sanctuary, his safe haven. It's a place where he can be at peace, hide from the rest of the world and read about the latest technological breakthrough in magnetic bait cast reels in *Field & Stream.*

Also there's a lock on the door and *you* can't get at him. If he runs the water hard enough he can even drown out the sound of your voice hollering at him through the door.

Does this mean that married men hiding from their wives are the only ones who worship for hours at the porcelain altar? Not at all. Men need to feel comfortable and relaxed to enjoy a bowel movement and will go to extraordinary lengths to achieve this comfort. Even if it means locking their sphincter muscles for an entire ten day trip. That's why lots of men in vacation spots tend to walk funny.

Most men even have a favorite time to go. As a matter of fact, most men's systems are so finely calibrated that you can set your watch by their daily constitutional. They **must** go at the same time every day **no matter where they are**. So they cultivate a number of favorite, strategically located potties, special spots where they can feel at home. Like the bathroom at work (for when he's at the office), the john at the coffee shop (for when he's on the road), his favorite home bathroom (for when he's at home), behind the blue spruce near the twelfth green (for when he's on the golf course), etc., etc.

That's why the key to the executive bathroom has always been a sign of true prestige and power. Once a man has access to these hallowed stalls he is privy (yes, I know that's a horrendous pun, but I couldn't help it) to the true inner workings of big business. Women executives can gain access to all the exclusive athletic clubs and country clubs they like, but until they figure out how to get next to the CEO as he takes his morning crap, they'll remain on the outside. The power lunch is nothing compared to the power poop.

A MAN'S LIBRARY

A man learns early in life that his home is his castle, he is king, and that a king's place is on the throne. The throne-sitting ritual gives him comfort and peace and affords him a chance to catch up on his reading. The following is a list of the most read bathroom periodicals for men of all ages.

AGES	IN THE BATHROOM
5 to 10	Hilights, Dr. Suess
11 to 16	Mad, Creem
17 to 20	Playboy, National Lampoon
21 to 25	Penthouse, Car & Driver
26 to 35	Sports Illustrated, Esquire, GQ
36 to 45	Field & Stream, Guns & Ammo
46 to 55	Consumer Reports, Health
56 to 65	Golf, Golf Digest, Golf Illustrated
66 & Over	Reader's Digest

Q. Why is it that men constantly seem to want to, uh...touch themselves, you know what I mean?

A. I think what you're referring to is the habit many men have of readjusting the old "package" from time to time. Some men do this because they're uncomfortable, some because they're actually in pain and some because they just like to check around in that area once in a while to make sure it's still there.

Many women are appalled by this sort of behavior but some understanding is called for here. Unfortunately for men, custom dictates that they wear pants. And for humans with external reproductive organs, pants are extremely impractical things to wear. Trousers were probably designed by the same guy who designed men's bicycles *with* the top bar instead of without. A woman can never know the agony a young man feels the first time he misjudges the height of a steep curb while riding a man's bike. Ugh.

Sad to say, this weird fashion thing got started a long time ago and it's too late to do anything about it now, but the fact is, when it comes to trousers, men get a (literally) raw deal. Unless they're Scottish.

Q. Everywhere I look these days I see men with long sideburns or raggedy beards or drooping mustaches with food in them. What gives? I hope the fashions of the Sixties aren't returning.

A. A man's facial hair is as personal to him as a woman's fragrance is to her. A mustachioed man can spend hours in front of the mirror combing, trimming, plucking, stroking and fondling in wonderment the collection of hairs that has grown out of his face as if by magic. Heavily bearded men amuse themselves for years by trimming their facial hair in new and exciting ways, or by shaving and regrowing their beards again and again while their more downy cheeked pals look on in envy and wonderment.

It will do no good, by the way, to complain about your man's new growth. In it's early stages, a ragged beard makes a man feel rugged, like a frontiersman, even though it makes him look scruffy, like a wino. Later, as it fills in, a beard makes a man feel learned and wise. Bearded men often smoke pipes and talk at length about *Madame Bovary* and Flaubert's "motivation." Even men who have never read more than the classified ad section of the *National Enquirer* do this once they grow a beard.

Thankfully, we are living in a time when almost all forms of decorative facial hair are considered gauche and truly unfashionable for men. Not that this stops too damn many of them. Unfortunate men who cling to the notion that "mutton chop" sideburns and "Fu Manchu" mustaches are still all the rage need to be taken aside and whispered to gently in a manner normally reserved for a friend at a dinner party with a bit of food stuck in her teeth. It may do no good but you'll feel better for having made the effort.

Q. What is the deal with men and their cars? My boyfriend would rather spend his days off rubbing his car with a diaper than spend them with me!

A. As I said, modern science has yet to come up with a fool-proof method for penis enlargement, although a friend of mine once sent away for a product that was sort of a weighted donut designed to be hung on the penis to supposedly lengthen it. (He swears he never used it but he did spend a good deal of our junior year in high school walking with a strange sort of limp). Because of this, men ease their feelings of inadequacy by means of **The Phallic Symbol**. A phallic symbol can be any male possession that expresses a man's power and machismo. Can't be any doubt as to what Trump Tower stands for, eh Donald?

Q. But why cars in particular?

A. Since large, penis-shaped skyscrapers are beyond the means of most men, they have to make do with that most classic of all American phallic symbols, the automobile.

A man can drive as big and as long and as powerful a car as he can afford. He is not forced to putter around in some tiny, economy model just because Mother Nature has capriciously foisted one upon him. For men, a powerful, sleek and shiny automobile can be extremely erotic.

Pshaw, you say? Think this car/penis theory is just so much pop psychobabble for the next Oprah show? ("Men Who Love Their Cars And The Women Who Love Them, tomorrow at nine!") Oh yeah? Tell me what man doesn't get a sexual thrill riding through the drive-through car wash? Ever watch a man spend an hour washing his prized sports car with special soap and special rags and then another hour gently but firmly rubbing wax up and down and up and down the finish? Why, some men even tape full color centerfolds of their favorite hot cars on the wall of their garage so they can fantasize while they rub.

If a man gets really wealthy he can afford to have other men wash and rub and drive his car *for* him. Imagine the psychological implications of *that.*

Q. What in the world makes a grown adult man think it's acceptable behavior to spit in public?

A. Well, for one thing, Joe Montana does it. A man's desire to emulate professional athletes knows no bounds. It may seem strange to you that a 41-year-old adult wears a $100 real-authentic-just-like-the-pros-wear football jersey around with a 22-year-old running back's name on it, but that's because *you* don't understand the attachment a man feels to sport. (*You* wear clothing and perfumes because famous, marginally talented television actresses and pop singers do, though, don't you?).

It seems that the abnormally active glands that cause professional sportsmen and athletes to grow into such big doofy guys also produce prodigious amounts of saliva. Some jocks even develop the habit of chewing on large wads of tobacco to help them produce even more spit. All this stuff has to go somewhere and hey, why not load a chunk on your tongue and blast it across the field, hmm? Athletes are very competitive of course, and some become so good at spitting that they run training facilities in the off season for novices.

Since life is a sporting event to many men (and not a cabaret, ol' chum as some would have you believe), they often feel the need to spit. It's sort of a male communication device. Oftentimes people use body language as a sort of communication shorthand, using a hand gesture, say, to indicate that they're finished speaking or to stress a point. Spitting is used by men in much the same way. "I landed the Andersen account today," your man will say as you walk towards a fine restaurant, and then he'll launch a glob of phlegm ten feet into the street with a loud "thwap" as a sort of proud exclamation point. This is normal for men and you should try not to gag.

SOME UGLY TRUTHS ABOUT MEN

1. They say they'll call and they don't.

2. They say "I love you" and they don't mean it.

3. They forget your birthday.

4. They forget your anniversary.

5. They forget Valentine's Day.

6. They *never* forget when *you* make a mistake.

7. Or when baseball season starts.

8. They snore.

9. They hog the covers.

10. They spit.

Section Two

THE MYSTERIOUS WORLD OF MALE BONDING

Behind the Locker Room Door

Q. Why do men have to spend so much time together? I mean, what is the deal with all this beer drinking and cigar smoking and belching and farting?

A. A man needs his buddies in a way that few women can ever understand. By the time *you* come into his life, a man will have spent countless hours with his pals drinking heavily in bars, staggering through the streets singing obscene fraternity songs, and barfing on the ground behind garbage dumpsters. These are things that women rarely get together to do.

Men love to scamper around grassy fields with other men, leaping and cavorting and patting one another on the butt. This is called "athletic competition" and is not to be referred to as "latent homosexuality."

There are many things that a man just doesn't feel comfortable discussing with a woman, things he can discuss only with another of his sex. Things like stock car racing, country music and professional midget wrestling, for example. *Women* always seem to want to talk about love, relationships, intimacy and (ugh, the 'C' word) commitment. You know, "girl stuff." This kind of talk often causes a man to turn pale and sickly and race into the bathroom for an hour or two with the *Sports Illustrated* Swimsuit issue.

Q. What, exactly, goes on at a bachelor party?

A. The bachelor party is a crucial cog in the huge male bonding machine. It is a culmination of all the things a man feels he is leaving behind as he renounces the joys of bachelorhood, i.e., the drinking, the camaraderie, the drinking, the carousing, the drinking, the cheap, sleazy one-night stands, and the drinking.

The average bachelor party begins with several hours of (can you guess?) drinking, card playing, belching and farting out loud, and watching videocassettes of pale, naked men and women with tattoos licking each other and moaning.

It is, in short, a blissful celebration of maleness. After a few hours of these shenanigans, it's time for the main event. A live nude woman! The stripper is usually a rather large breasted, gelatinous woman with thighs the texture of orange rinds, who strips to supplement her real career as a gas station attendant.

The guest of honor will take a seat in the center of the room so the stripper can dance around him, twirl her breasts in large circles and grind her privates into his face to the tune of Madonna's "Like A Virgin." For men, this is highly refined entertainment. As breasts twirl and crotches grind, they mix up exotic cocktails with names like "Silk Panty" and "Screaming Orgasm" and force them on the grinning groom. They slap him on the back and shout words of encouragement like "Well, buddy, looks like those carefree bachelor days are over for good!" and "It's not too late to back out yet, ha ha!"

After the stripper leaves and the final toasts are drunk, it's time for traditional male bachelor party hijinks. You see, once a large group of males get a load of alcohol and testosterone dumped into their systems they need an outlet, a way to work off a little steam. Like dropping the semi-conscious groom naked into a boxcar bound for Saskatoon. The details of these wacky hijinks are too scary to retell but suffice it to say that they frequently involve public nudity, fist fights and jail time. (Actually, I wouldn't mind telling about the rest of the details of a typical bachelor party but I can never remember any).

Q. That is the sickest thing I ever heard! How come bachelor parties aren't against the law?

A. Most women, I know, find the bachelor party in all its glorious tradition to be gross, crass, base, crude, disgusting and contemptible. It is, of course, all of these things. What women don't seem to understand is that the true function of the bachelor party is not to break down the sacred trust of marriage but to *preserve* it.

You see, when the poor groom-to-be wakes up naked, in a puddle of frozen vomit on the floor of an ice cold boxcar speeding through Hibbing, Minnesota, he will forget all about any misgivings he may have still had about his impending nuptials. With a headache that would kill a bull elephant and the dim memory (and fragrance) of an overweight stripper's bushy crotch pounding in his brain, he will weep gratefully when his lovely bride-to-be comes to take him home.

After this little lesson in bachelorhood gone mad, the prospective groom will be quiet, thoughtful and obedient (not to mention hung over) for weeks to come. He will pray for his wedding day to arrive so he no longer has to subject himself to such trauma.

This is the natural societal function the bachelor party fulfills.

It makes marriage look *damn* good.

Q. What goes on inside a men's locker room? Is it true they actually shower together and stuff? That's so gross!

A. What goes on in a men's locker room is pretty much the same stuff that goes on in a women's locker room. It just smells worse. And it *is* true that most men's showers are communal, but that's okay because men *enjoy* group nudity. They enjoy parading around in brightly lit locker rooms, and lounging in foggy, flatulence-filled saunas naked with other naked men.

Men find a woman's need for privacy strange. Which is why if you live with a man, it's always better to have separate bathrooms. Unless you think you'll enjoy the sight of him sitting on the john while you brush your teeth.

THINGS MEN TALK ABOUT IN THE LOCKER ROOM

1. **Sex**

2. **Sports**

3. **Cars**

4. **Business**

And actually, they don't really talk about the last three that much.

Q. My husband goes on hunting trips with his friends all the time. What possible enjoyment could come from such a thing?

A. Man was born to hunt. The need to pit himself against the elements, the desire to match wits with cunning and elusive wildlife, the primal urge to commune with nature, these are the things which stir a hunter's soul each fall and cause him to polish his rifle and march off to strange, faraway lands. Like Wisconsin, for instance. That, and the desire to power down some brewskis and play with guns.

Men *love* to play with guns. As children, they naturally gravitate away from sedate, gentle games like "Hopscotch" or "Playing House" to games like "Let's Poke Someone's Eye Out With A Pointed Stick" and "Dirt Clod Death Ambush." But these children's games are, due to local legislation, almost always non-fatal. Imagine the thrill an adult male must feel when he finally gets the opportunity to really murder a living being!

Men have a natural affinity and a deep kinship with wild animals and nature. They long to sleep on the ground, to go without bathing for days at a time and to go to the bathroom out of doors. They respect and revere the dignity of the leaping deer and the soaring dove. They long to live like these beautiful creatures, to think like them and to become one with them.

And to mercilessly slaughter them with sophisticated automatic weapons.

MALE BONDING RITUAL #23
"The Hunting Trip"

SOME MORE UGLY TRUTHS ABOUT MEN

1. They tickle you until you scream.

2. They leave the seat up.

3. They leave the seat down, and pee on it.

4. They think stretch marks are funny.

5. They don't understand shopping.

6. They drive like maniacs.

7. They won't admit it when they're lost.

8. They never listen.

9. When they *do* listen they hear the wrong things.

10. They buy drinks for total strangers.

Section Three

MAN'S BEST FRIEND
Auto-Eroticism

A man will go through many changes during his life. He'll have several jobs, travels and experiences, but one thing will remain constant: the deep and abiding love he feels for his automobiles. From the first beater a man buys as a teen-ager to the luxury sports model he buys when having his mid-life crisis, a man and his car have a bond that goes beyond words.

To a man, a car isn't just transportation. His car is a statement. It doesn't say who he is. It is much more important. It says *who he wants to be.* For that reason, a car reveals everything about a man. Different men buy different cars for different reasons, but every man will own these six sooner or later: his **First Car, Sports Car, Company Car, Family Car, "I Got Mine" Car** and his **Retirement Car**.

A man's **First Car** is a lot like his first love. He never quite gets over either one. And he probably still carries pictures of both in his wallet. **First Cars** are overwhelmingly American models, either huge, rattling Pontiacs or squeaking, rusting Fords. A man/boy buys his first car as a symbol of his manhood. He reads *Road & Track* magazine, he discusses the merits of various engine block sizes with friends, he visits dozens of car lots and reads all the ads in the Sunday paper. And he still ends up buying the most dangerous, rusted hulk in a four-state area.

As ugly a beast as a first auto often is, most men love it with a devotion akin to what they feel for *Gilligan's Island* reruns. They spend hours slathering corroded quarter panels with Bondo and touch-up paint. They painstakingly cover tired seats and rotted floor boards with carpet remnants. And they spend every penny they have on an elaborate sound system with enough power to stun a water buffalo at several hundred feet. Most first cars are not so much automobiles as they are speakers with wheels.

A man buys a **Sports Car** for many reasons. Most have terrific cornering ability, great handling and get excellent gas mileage. Mostly, though, men buy a sports car to get babes. It's the same as learning to play guitar except you don't get blisters.

The proper **Sports Car** will have an engine that sounds as though someone at the plant forgot to attach the muffler. It will be named for some vicious predatory animal and have several meaningless numbers tacked on after the name, like *"Mako Shark 7200/99XLT."*

Seemingly normal men turn into crazed macho pigs when behind the wheel of such a car. Mild mannered accountants blast brazenly through red lights. Easygoing banking executives roar down the expressway at 110 miles per hour, eyes glued to the tachometer screaming "This baby's got plenty left!" Thank God the good people in the insurance industry have jacked their rates up so high that it's almost impossible for the average guy to own a sports car anymore. They're always looking out for us, aren't they?

Once a man settles down, "gets done sowing his wild oats," and basically gives up having fun forever, he must enter the working world. This usually involves getting a job selling something people don't really need, which is a tough gig. To do this properly he must have a respectable (i.e. boring) car. Thank goodness most forward-thinking companies provide **Company Cars** for their sales people these days. God knows no one else would buy them.

The only trouble with a **Company Car** is that when he wrecks it on the way back from a Sunday barbecue with his softball buddies he has to figure out how to get the insurance people to believe that it was somehow business related. Luckily, insurance companies make plenty of money gouging **Sports Car** drivers so they don't mind being lied to once in awhile by **Company Car** drivers.

Once a man has married and has some kiddies, he often realizes the need for more substantial transportation. He may be able to sell the boss a couple of weekend fender-benders but there's no way to explain how an important client left a pizza box from "Chuck E Cheese" in the back seat. Now's the time a man trusts his fathering instincts and purchases the **Family Car.** He'll remember all those swell car trips he took as a kid, being car sick and throwing up out the window, peeing in a coffee can because Dad's fed up with stopping "every goddamn half-hour." Yes, all those wonderful memories will come flooding back to him like raw sewage. He'll undoubtedly choose a nice station wagon, or, the modern equivalent, the Mini-Van, a curious vehicle designed by Japanese auto manufacturers who wanted to see just how ugly they could make a car before Americans stopped buying them by the millions.

After his family is raised, his wife divorced, and his drinking problem is fully matured, the American male will want to make a statement about himself. He'll want to announce to the world that he's made it to the top of the corporate heap, that his life is a shambles, his kids hate him, the IRS is after his business and that his former mistress is threatening to have a chat with Kitty Kelly. And what better way to do that than by buying the biggest, most impractical, tasteless, out-dated, ridiculously expensive vehicle possible? Thus, the **"I Made It" Car**, suitable for parking at fancy country clubs, formal charity events and Congressional Ethics Committee hearings.

Finally, a man needs a **Retirement Car**, a car he can drive to the grave. Or to Miami Beach, which is pretty much the same thing. He'll like the comfort and safety of a big huge car at this age, something made with lots of steel. A ponderous beast with cruise control so he can catch short catnaps on the drive to the golf course every day.

These are just a few examples of the major automobile purchases a man makes in a lifetime. There are so many others. The **"Mid-Life Crisis" Convertible**, the **"Marlboro Man" Jeep**, the **"Fixer-Upper"** restore job, and many, many more. Remember to be understanding with a man and his car obsession. He buys a car when he wants to feel good, when he wants to make a statement, when he wants to change his life and, sometimes, just for the hell of it. It's the same relationship women have with shoes.

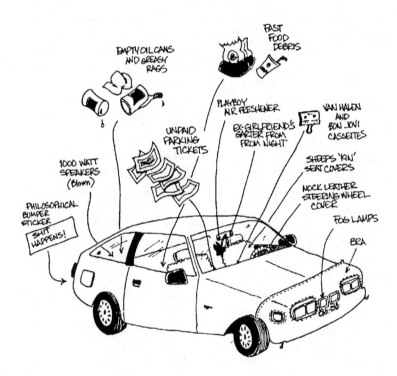

HIS FIRST CAR

Make:
Ford, Chevy, Pontiac, etc.
Anything that weighs at least 4 tons.

Year:
Anything made around the same year the buyer was born.

Inside:
Shag carpet remnants to cover holes in floorboards. Prom date's garter on rearview mirror.

Outside:
Loose molding. Missing hubcaps.

Colors:
Primer Gray. Undercoat Red. Rust Brown.

Options:
"Leather look" steering wheel cover. "Sheep's Kin" seat covers.

In Glove Box:
Unpaid tickets. Condoms.

Radio:
10,000 watts of rock and roll power, baby.

Speed:
Cruising at 12 mph.
Slower if babes are present.

Bumper Sticker:
"Shit Happens."

HIS SPORTS CAR

Make:
Any car named for an animal except the Pinto.

Year:
Very new. "Vintage" vehicles are acceptable if they are fully restored and souped up.

Inside:
Lots of leather.

Outside:
Pin stripes. Mag wheels. Chrome bumpers. Bra. Fog lamps.

Colors:
Red or black only.

Options:
Real leather steering wheel cover. Real sheepskin seat covers. Fuzz-buster.

In Glove Box:
Extra bottle of Armor-All. "New Car" scent air freshener. Unpaid tickets. Condoms.

Radio:
European-made CD player stereo system including 24 band equalizer.

Speed:
Yes.

Bumper Stickers:
"I Can't Drive 55"

"I ♥ My 640XZ 7000LT4"

HIS COMPANY CAR

Make:
All company cars for the past few years have been Chrysler K Cars. It's one of those deals Iaccoca made with the government.

Year:
Who knows? They're all the same.

Inside:
Cigarette butts from the last guy who had it. Vinyl and plastic.

Outside:
Dents and nicks from the last guy who had it. Black sidewall tires.

Colors:
Beige. Occasionally Powder Blue.

Options:
Suction cup note pad on dash and non-spill, insulated, free-refill, convenience store coffee cup.

In Glove Box:
Street map of sales area. Rolaids. Tums. Alka Seltzer. Certs.

Radio:
Delco AM radio. Tuned to all-news station.

Speed:
Completely reckless. It's not his car.

Bumper Sticker:
"Please Report Unsafe Driving to 634-5789"

HIS FAMILY CAR

Make:
Station Wagon or Mini-Van.

Year:
As new as he can afford.

Inside:
Spilled ice cream. Screaming children.

Outside:
Bike racks. Fake wooden side panels.

Colors:
Any color that hides dirt.

Options:
Century 2000 kiddie car seat.

In Glove Box:
Crumpled fast food bags.
Improperly folded maps. Moist towelettes.
Kleenex travel packs. Old popsicle sticks.

Radio:
Factory installed AM/FM cassette deck with "Raffi's Baby Beluga" cassette permanently wedged in it.

Speed:
Slow in school zones when children present.

Bumper Sticker:
"Baby on Board"

HIS "I GOT MINE" CAR

Make:
Cadillac, Lincoln, Mercedes.

Year:
Next year's model, this year.

Inside:
Corinthian leather.

Outside:
Tinted windows, hood ornament.

Colors:
Black.

Options:
All of them.

In Glove Box:
Nothing.

Radio:
Elevator music.

Speed:
Relaxed. Everybody will wait.

Bumper Sticker:
Country Club parking permit.

HIS RETIREMENT CAR

Make:
Any vehicle with the approximate wheel base and weight of an aircraft carrier.

Year:
They don't make 'em like this any more!

Inside:
Compass on dash next to St. Christopher statue.

Outside:
Fins.

Colors:
Lemon Yellow, Lime Green and any other color no one else with a complete range of vision would want.

Options:
Power everything.

In Glove Box:
Metamucil.

Radio:
Paul Harvey.

Speed:
Never above the posted minimum.

Bumper Sticker:
"Ask About My Grandchildren!"
"Yellowstone National Park"
"See Rock City"
"Tommy Bartlett's Water Show"

BOY, I HOPE IT DOESN'T RAIN TONIGHT,
WHAT WITH MY BRAND NEW PORSCHE
PARKED OUT IN THE OPEN AND ALL !

HE IS WHAT HE DRIVES

A List of Autos and Their Owners

Audi:
Not a doctor yet, but he will be soon.

BMW:
Same as above. Can substitute lawyer or accountant for doctor.

Buick Electra:
He smokes a cigar, is at least 48 years old. Wishes he could afford a Cadillac.

Buick (other):
A solid American guy. Likes vanilla ice cream. Wonders what Dolly Parton looks like naked.

Blazer:
He fancies himself a great outdoorsman but doesn't like to get his hair mussed by driving a Jeep.

Cadillac:
He's made enough money to buy whatever he wants, so he buys the car his Dad would have loved.

Camaro:
He likes to play the stereo loud.
Wishes Led Zepplin would get back together.
Calls women "chicks." Even his Mom.

Celica:
A young professional. Has enough money to get deeply in debt, but not yet enough to get in debt for a Porsche.

Cherokee:
See Blazer.

Civic:
He is practical. Wears glasses. Enjoys coin or stamp collecting. Frequently says "I'm not cheap. I'm frugal."

Corvette:
Wears leather jacket. And Old Spice. And several gold chains. Subscribes to Penthouse. A mouth breather.

Dodge (any):
He is your Dad, or someone else's. Believes in "Buying American." Likes call-in radio shows. Still owns a CB.

Firebird:
Just like the Corvette driver only without the sense of style.

Ford (any):
See Dodge (any).

Honda Accord:
Smug. Spouts Consumer Reports statistics about customer satisfaction and product reliability. Has paid up service contracts on every major appliance. Orders all his clothes from "Land's End" catalogs.

Jeep:
Thinks he's the Marlboro Man. Wears jeans and down vests a lot. Plows driveways in the winter for extra cash.

Mercedes:
Made his pile, but he's not ready for the chauffeured limo yet. Likes to do business on his car phone. He's married, but he'll still buy you lunch.

Mustang (pre-'68):

Going through his "second chilhood." Remembers all the words to "American Pie" and knows what they mean.

New Yorker:

He is Ricardo Montalban.

Nova:

He is unstable. Frequently on unemployment. May machine-gun a post office at anytime.

Oldsmobile (any):

See Dodge (any) and Ford (any).

Pick Up Truck:

Chews tobacco. Spits frequently. Owns several weapons. Wadrobe consists almost entirely of T-shirts with obscenities on them.

Spyder:

Thinks he's James Dean. Do not go for a spin around the block with this man.

Trans-Am:
Same as Corvette only without the sense of style or taste.

VW Bug:
Wears wire rimmed glasses, Hush Puppies and carries a back pack. Graduate student in archaic subject. Vegetarian.

VW Bus:
Thinks it's 1969. Smokes lots of dope. Sells peanut butter sandwiches and tie-dyed T-shirts at Grateful Dead concerts.

Section Four

THE DATING GAME
The Relationship Problem

Q. How is it that every time I go out on a date with a man he feels as though it's an invitation to jump my bones?

A. Most men have very simple tastes. They firmly believe that dating should be a trade-off, kind of a business transaction. A man figures that if he buys a woman a Whopper and a chocolate shake and takes her to a movie she ought to be up for a night of wild, unbridled passion. And he'll be hurt to the core if she isn't. More interestingly, he'll even be puzzled by this sort of behavior.

It's not that a man resents paying for dinner and a show. He realizes that it's part of the deal. Most don't even mind a little intelligent conversation if it's completely necessary. He'd just like a little assurance that he'll eventually end up with a nice payoff. That is, that the evening will end up with him gasping and flopping on top of you like a Big Mouth Bass with a hook in its mouth.

Of course, not *all* men are this unsophisticated. Some wouldn't think of entertaining a lady with anything less than dinner at an elegant restaurant, front-row seats at a popular theatrical production and perhaps a horse drawn carriage ride at the end of the evening. These men are generous. They are well spoken. They are intelligent and thoughtful. They also figure that a woman's more likely to come across this way.

Q. Why do men like to date more than one woman at a time? Does it make them feel like they've got some sort of harem or something?

A. In a word, yes. Men have little interest in quality when it comes to dating. They're interested in quantity. You might think of a man's social life as one of those huge fund raising thermometer signs that stand outside smalltown city halls and Chambers of Commerce growing taller and redder as each pledge dollar comes in. (Men's lives are just chock-full of phallic metaphors just as stupid and obvious as that one).

Once a man reaches his personal pledge goal, or just gets tired of tawdry, shallow romances, he may actually begin to mature enough to finally desire a truly giving, passionate, healthy, committed one-on-one relationship with a woman. But don't hold your breath.

Q. Every decent looking man I see these days seems to be with a woman half his age with huge hair and huge boobs. Do I have to be stupid to get a date?

A. No, but it doesn't hurt.

TEN REASONS
MEN DATE BIMBOS

1. They're easily impressed.

2. They're easy to be with.

3. They're easy to entertain.

4. They're easy on the eyes.

5. They're easy to talk to.

6. They're easily amused.

7. They're easy to find.

8. They're easy to travel with.

9. They're easy to get rid of.

10. They're easy.

Q. If, after a date, I go up to a man's apartment with him, will he expect me to...uh..."go all the way?"

A. "Go all the way?"..."Go all the way?" What in the heck kind of wimpy expression is that? What you're asking is, if you go back to a man's apartment after he's spent the better part of two weeks' pay feeding you, entertaining you and plying you with alcohol will he expect you to "make the Beast with Two Backs?" ('Beast with Two Backs,' now there's a euphemism!).

The answer is, *of course he will.* When a man asks you up to his apartment what he is asking in Malespeak is not "Do you want to come up for a chat and a cup of coffee?" He's asking, "Do you want to make the 'Beast with Two Backs?" (Boy, I love that expression).

If you accept this invitation, he has every reason to expect you to "put out." (That's the euphemism Grandpa always used. Don't ask me how I know.)

Not for a moment am I suggesting that a lady *ever* trade her favors for a night out with a gentleman. Never would I suggest that you should be expected to compromise yourself for dinner and a few drinks!

However, if he throws in flowers and a nice gift...

TEN MEN TO AVOID
IN THE DATING POOL

1. Men who wear gold chains.

2. Men who smoke thin, brown French cigarettes.

3. Men with sideburns that exceed 4 inches.

4. Balding men who comb long strands of their remaining hair across the top of their head.

5. Men who speak of their ex-wives' sexual shortcomings in colorful detail.

6. Men who order for you in restaurants.

7. Professional clowns.

8. Men with visible nose hair.

9. Men who live with their mothers.

10. Men with tattoos.

IS HE RELATIONSHIP MATERIAL?

A Test

It's often difficult to determine whether or not a man has **Relationship Potential** or not. Introducing him to your Mom is a good test. If she likes him, he's probably a disaster. If that is inconvenient for you, use this one. See how the man whose potential you wish to assess fares based on the following five **MAN QUALITIES.**

MONEY
(or "Earning Potential").

LOOKS
*(If he has Tom Cruise's smile
who cares about anything else?).*

TASTE
*(Could you really love a man
who collects Redd Foxx Albums?).*

FAMILY
*(Is his maternal grandfather bald?
His maternal grandmother?).*

MONEY
*(I know I mentioned this one already
but let's not kid ourselves, it makes up
for a lot).*

Rate the man in question in each of the five categories on a scale from one to twenty. Total all scores. This will give you a final score of between zero and one hundred.

The following is a sample test just to make it clear.

Sylvester Stallone

Say you're lunching with your agent at Spago when that kicky little red outfit you just bought catches the Slyster's eye. He is entranced by your wit and your perfume. He begs you to dine with him at his palatial Malibu beach house. Do you? Use the **Relationship Potential Test** to decide!

MONEY: 20 points
(Say what you want about ol' Sly, but he hauls in big dough.)

LOOKS: 15 points
(Some women go for the 'Prince of Pecs' and some don't.)

TASTE: 4 points
(This is the guy who made the movie FIST.)

FAMILY: 2 points
(The man has Brigitte Nielsen for an ex-wife and a mother who manages lady wrestlers.)

MONEY: 4 points
(He'd probably make you sign a pre-nuptial agreement anyway.)

So, old Sly gets a measly 45 on our hundred-point scale. (See following). That drops him into the definitely questionable range. I'd say if you are desperately bored, have absolutely no plans on Saturday and Stallone calls, then go for it. Otherwise you're probably better off staying home with a good book.

THE GRADING SCALE

85 to 100
Have this man's child. Immediately if possible. He is perfect for you. Your mother will like him, your friends will be jealous and old boyfriends will call you on the phone weeping and gnashing their teeth.

60 to 84
This man has definite potential. Move him away from his mother. Buy him some decent clothing. He is probably aware that there are some restaurants that serve food not wrapped in paper, though he may not have actually ever been to one. Take him.

45 to 59
We're talking borderline here. Only date this man if you're really lonely, really bored, or if he has lots and lots of money.

30 to 44

I'm ashamed of you for even considering this man. He is a warm body but not much more. He owns at least three polyester sport coats and one of them is robin's egg blue.

15 to 29

This man is not for you unless you have several large tattoos and you work selling chili dogs out of a small trailer in Tijuana.

0 to 14

This man began walking upright only about six weeks ago. He is probably a hockey fan.

Q. Jeez, are there any good men around anymore?

A. Well, no, there aren't really. There is a terrific man who lives in Missouri who's just about to become divorced but if I publish his name he'll be swamped by tens of thousands of eager women and I don't think the expressways of that state could take it.

Section Five

SEX AND THE MODERN MAN
Much Ado About Nothing

Q. If you ask me, most men have a weird fascination with their, well, you know...their things. Why is this?

A. The thing about men is, they're born with penises. Most of them are, anyway. (That's the word by the way, "penis." I know it's a scary one but let's try to be adult here, eh?). And because of this, they're born into a kind of slavery that women can never truly understand. Scientists know very little about these cunning little items but apparently, they prevent human beings from thinking at all clearly. It seems that a large part of a man's brain (the part responsible for love, decency and rational thought) is governed by chemical reactions controlled directly by his penis! Indeed, a man with a raging erection will dress in a chicken suit and jump in front of a freight train if he thinks it will bring sexual relief.

Freud theorized that many of the difficulties between men and women were caused by a malady he described as "penis envy." He figured that having a penis was such a swell deal that anyone who didn't have one (that's you, ladies) must be insane with jealousy.

As is the case with so many men, when it comes to sex, Freud didn't have a clue. However keen *men* may think it is to have a penis, *women* no more wish to acquire one than they wish to acquire a pre-frontal lobotomy or weeping dermatitis. Women are far too intelligent to covet an appendage that clearly creates an uncontrollable urge to purchase expensive, gaudy jewelry for women named "Queenie" who wear gold lame tube tops and hang out in bars.

Q. Why is the size of his penis such a big deal to a man?

A. Well, actually, sometimes it's kind of a *small* deal! Ha Ha! (Look, don't expect cutting edge humor for this price). There are only four men in the entire world who feel that their penises aren't too small. And they're all making films in dingy West Hollywood apartments with large- breasted women which will later be shown at a bachelor party.

You see, men feel that no matter what they've accomplished in their lives, they know that to feel *really* manly and successful requires a huge wiener. A man feels that if he is a less than fabulous lover it's because he's just not big enough. "Forget about that troublesome old foreplay," thinks the hapless male, "forget about romance, warmth, love and affection! I'll bet if I had a twelve-inch wangeroo she'd be happy!" If you think breast enlargements are popular just wait until some pioneering plastic surgeon invents a method for penis enlargement that really works. The entire male population will be standing in line.

And when you break up with a man, he'll know just exactly why. It won't be because he rarely remembered your birthday, because he made fun of your thighs, because he barfed on your mother's shoes at your sister's wedding or because his little pet name for you is "Blubber Butt." No indeed. These are all simply feeble feminine excuses designed to cover up the ugly truth.

WELL, YOU KNOW WHAT THEY SAY, "IT'S NOT THE SIZE OF THE WAVE, IT'S THE MOTION OF THE OCEAN!"

No matter what you say, he'll look at you reproachfully and say "So, you found a guy with a bigger schlong, eh?"

Q. What is the deal with those "girlie" magazines? Why do men find them so captivating? Live women too intimidating? Afraid they won't be able to handle a woman with a brain and a body? Are the pictures just safer or what?!

A. My, my, hostile aren't we? Just make a little surprise discovery about a loved one's reading habits? Don't sweat it, babe. *Every* man has a little collection of magazines around for those long, cold winter nights when there's nobody around to whip him with a rolled up paper and call him "Sparky."

Men are practical creatures when it comes to their libidinous urges and nothing is more comforting to a man than knowing that the "Girls of Pig's Eye, Arkansas" are waiting, warm, moist and willing, safe on the bottom of his sock drawer.

A man loves his friendly little naked lady pictures because they never talk back, they never develop rippling cellulite, they have no irritating in-laws, they don't demand two hours of that tedious old foreplay, they always let him leave the light on and *they're always in the mood.*

Bob Guccione isn't worth millions because he publishes government exposes or essays by William F. Buckley. He made his pile printing full-color photos of blow-dried, air-brushed, cap-

toothed, bare-ass naked teen-age girls squirting baby oil on one another.

Heck, let your man keep his little secret library in his sock drawer. Isn't that where you stash your vibrator?

Q. Before we were married, my husband was after me for sex all the time. Now, I practically have to drag him into the bedroom. What's the deal?

A. The thing about men is they're born hunters driven by their urges to stalk and conquer. Men desire sex because it means they played a game and won. Kind of like getting a bowling trophy. Making love because it's a beautiful expression of passion and commitment is a truly bizarre concept for a man to digest and the suggestion of such a thing will make him scratch his chin and belch quizzically.

Once the hunt is over, I'm afraid, a man's urges may diminsh considerably. As a friend of mine once said to me "Hell, even golf would get boring if you had to play the same hole every day." Clearly, this kind of comment is *completely* objectionable and I won't even dignify it with a response.

The sick part of all this is that just about the time most men's urges are on the decline, many women begin to want to buy slinky lingerie, erotic videotapes and silk whips. There is no scientific reason for this, it's just one of Mother Nature's little pranks.

Luckily for our species, men's and women's sex drives *do* match up for awhile. This usually happens for about six or eight days during our late twenties. If not for this short period of time, the human race would certainly have become extinct eons ago.

(Imagine, *golf* getting boring! Hah!)

Q. So how can I get him to shut off Letterman for awhile and get him to pay some attention to me?

A. Try this: Put on some lacy "Fredericks of Hollywood" underwear, garter belt and stockings, high heels, and musky perfume. Then, stroll into the bedroom, switch off the television and say "Hi, big guy, I'm Mona the Man Eater and I can suck a tennis ball through a garden hose." If that doesn't work, he's a lost cause. But hell, things could be worse. He could be watching *The Cajun Chef.*

Q. Why are men so clumsy when it comes to making love? Don't any of them have a clue about a woman's physical needs?

A. Most men are truly mystified by just what in the hell it is that women want from the sex act. Men think of sex as a good time, all right (especially playing the "Enema Nurse and Reluctant Patient" game), but it's not up there with covering the point spread on every game in the office football pool or anything.

Sexually speaking, all men's equipment operates in similar fashion. Tab A goes into Slot B, wham, bam, thank you ma'am. Men envy women for this. They think that for a woman to be good in bed she just has to show up and be mildly interested for a minute or two.

Men face a much more formidable task when it comes to satisfying a woman sexually. They've all secretly read "Cosmopolitan" at the grocery check out counter. They know that, unlike a trusty outboard motor or a reliable chainsaw, every woman is supposedly *different*. Each one has separate and specific *needs*. But none of them come with an operator's manual! Nor do they want to come right out and say just what exactly goes where and when! Noooo, *that* would take all the romance out of it!

So, what happens? A man gets himself in a position to enjoy some safe and friendly boinking with a safe and friendly woman and he ends up struggling before her naked, prone form like a frustrated safecracker at the main vault of Fort Knox.

After years of this kind of struggle, mostmen figure it's just not worth the aggravation. They give up on sex with real live, hard-to-figure-out women and make do with "The Girls of Pig's Eye, Arkansas" stowed safely under their rolled up socks.

TEN "QUICK 'N' E-Z" SEXUAL SUBSTITUTES FOR A MAN

1. One gallon Haagen Daz Chocolate Mint Chip Ice Cream.

2. One week of "General Hospital" videotapes (Commercials removed.)

3. Ben Wa Balls.

4. A truly trashy little black dress.

5. The sequined pumps to match.

6. "Pocket Rocket" vibrator.

7. One Extra Large bag Nacho Cheese Doritos.

8. One pound Fannie Mae assorted chocolates.

9. A case of Tab.

10. A cucumber.

Q. Our sex life is okay, I guess, but I sure would like to get my husband to kiss me a little more often. Why does kissing lose its appeal for men?

A. Men are, I'm afraid, tremendously goal oriented. The dynamic drive that makes him yearn to be promoted from fry cook at McDonald's to full-fledged night manager is the same thing that makes him want to grope your privates only seconds after the smooching has begun.

I conducted a scientific poll (asking a few guys I met in a bar) and discovered the following: Given a choice, .04% of the men surveyed said they loved kissing more than any other form of sexual expression, 11% said it was better than a sock in the eye with a dead tuna, and 88.96% said "let's blow off this kissy-face garbage and get right to the good stuff!"

In fairness to the poor boys, you must keep in mind that these guys learned about sex in their girlfriend's basements with one ear and eye open, desperately hoping her folks weren't coming home. Speed was of the essence. This also may help explain what sex therapists refer to as "premature ejaculation," but I'm afraid that's a whole other book.

Q. Are all men obsessed with the size of a woman's breasts?

A. No, of course not. Some are obsessed with the shape of a woman's butt.

Q. Are all men obsessed with getting oral sex?

A. Yep.

SOME UGLY TRUTHS ABOUT MEN AND SEX

1. They want sex too often.

2. They don't want sex often enough.

3. They want weird sex.

4. They want sex at inconvenient times.

5. They brag about their sexual prowess.

6. They compare you with former lovers.

7. They eat in bed.

8. They fart in bed.

9. They fall asleep right after sex and snore like bulldozers.

10. They make you sleep in the wet spot.

Section Six

MARRYING A MAN
If You Still Feel You Must

Q. I've been dating my boyfriend for what seems like a million years. We're unofficially engaged, but I can't get him to set a date. What is this thing men have about commitment?

A. Men understand commitment. They just define it in different terms. To a man, commitment means making sure the VCR is set everyday to record "All-Star Wrestling." Commitment means keeping the same foursome and tee time together for ten years.

Thing of it is, Early Man lived in dangerous times. His life was constantly being threatened by ornery woolly mammoths, cranky sabre-toothed tigers and other Early Men armed with blunt instruments. Early Man's lifespan was sixteen or seventeen years at best. It's because of his ancestors that Modern Man has never developed the capacity to plan beyond the next several station breaks. Phrases like *"The Future"* and *"Til Death We Do Part"* and *"Diaper Pail"* are completely beyond his understanding and will likely make him pale with fright and tremble with apprehension.

So don't be too hard on the poor boys. Their forefathers spent most of their time hacking at underbrush and whacking at wild animals with sticks. That explains why they don't understand commitment. It also explains why they like golf so much.

(By the way, being 'unofficially engaged' is kind of like being unofficially pregnant. I mean, you *is* or you *ain't*).

Q. Okay, I understand that commitment is not a comfortable subject for him, so how do I get him to pop the question?

A. Men have a difficult time proposing marriage. It's just not something that they learn on the street corner. (Which is where they learn to do most of the other things that are important in life, like how to light Ohio Bluetip matches off the back of their teeth and how to make farting noises by squeezing one hand under the armpit). Left to his own devices, a man will rarely ask for your hand, though most have no trouble at all when it comes to asking for your other parts.

You see, men have a special language all their own, a language we social scientists call **"Malespeak."** (For more information on this phenomenon, see the test elsewhere in this book). The phrase "Will you marry me?" does not translate easily into the hard-to-fathom language of men. Roughly, it means "Will you drag me naked through a parking lot filled with broken glass?" Clearly, this is a difficult thing for a man to say with any real conviction.

Lots of women assume that what a man fears most in a proposal is rejection, so they seek to pave the way to marital bliss by making sure he knows that the answer to his proposal will be "Yes!" Ladies! Nothing could be further from the truth! "Yes, I will marry you" translates into Malespeak as "Not only will I drag you naked through a parking lot filled with broken glass, I will dip you in a vat of industrial solvent right afterward."

The best way to wring a proposal out of a reluctant suitor is to make sure he thinks the answer will be "No, not just yet, sweetie." Translation?: "No, I desire only to be your love slave and servant but I could never bear the responsibility of ending the freedom that I know a rugged, independent man like you craves. May I get you another beer, my master?"

Q. Oh, gag me. So why do men ever get married?

A. Mostly, to get some on a regular basis. No I'm just kidding. Actually, we already know what happens to the old sex life after marriage, don't we?

The real reason is that men are very competitive creatures and when they see that other men have wives, why, they decide that they better have one, too. That, and so they can have a bachelor party.

By the way, men like *long* engagements. Women often begin preparing for marriage somewhere around puberty when they receive their first subscription to *Bride's Magazine*. But a man generally needs some time to get used to the idea. The thought that he'll have to shut the door when he goes to the bathroom and pick up his dirty socks for the rest of his life sends many a man into a veritable tizzy. An engagement period of seven or eight years seems about right to most men, which works out well because that's about how long you'll need to reserve a nice hall and get a decent caterer.

The engagement period is also a time for a man to take stock of his life thus far and ponder the deep philosophical questions that we all must eventually confront. Questions like, "Why am I here?" And like, "What is the nature of love?" And like, "Is it too late to back out now?" And like "Is she gonna get as fat as her mother the minute we say 'I do'?"

These are the kinds of things men think of when they think of marriage. These things and football.

Q. What is it that a man expects from marriage?

A. Most men view a perfect marriage partner as a lifetime companion. A woman to warm them at night, to encourage them in the day, to fix oatmeal with brown sugar and cinnamon on top just like Mom used to do.

Don't be after a man to "open up" to you and reveal his "deepest emotions" unless you're prepared for the revelation that his deepest emotions involve whether or not the pork belly market has gone soft.

Men like the status quo. Once married, they like life to stay as it is. They have little interest in "growth" or deeper "communication." A man figures he should get what he bargains for in life and his wife is no exception. Should she put on a little weight or occasionally misplace her perky temperament, a man feels cheated and may begin rummaging through the junk drawer in search of a "wife warranty."

The life of Ben Cartwright is what every man dreams of. No one to pester him about his smelly boots or his frequent trips to Virginia City, an Oriental servant to cook simple food, and wives who stayed around just long enough to bear a son and then die tragically, long before they would have begun to nag him about building indoor plumbing or about his unnaturally close relationship with his horse.

Q. Aren't there some men who are just destined to be bachelors?

A. Yes, I'm afraid there are. If a man doesn't marry by the time he reaches his early thirties there's a very good chance he'll never marry at all. Oftentimes a man this age develops such weird habits that are so deeply ingrained that it would be almost impossible for another human being, particularly one who has no fondness for mildew, to live with him.

Usually, these men live in neat little studio apartments with a cleaning lady who comes twice a week. They often smoke pipes and frequently collect war memorabilia. Confirmed bachelors tend to drive expensive sports cars, wear little tweed caps and often have very small dogs for pets. You can see them out walking their poodles or dachshunds, smoking their pipes, wearing their caps and talking animatedly to the dog who will be wearing a sweater to match his owner's.

Confirmed bachelors are usually wild young men who become fussy middle-aged men who become dirty old men who become crazy old codgers. They tend to live into their nineties and spend their last years chugging around nursing homes in motorized wheel chairs lifting up nurses' skirts with their canes.

If you're a kid, though, it's neat to have a confirmed bachelor uncle because he'll always come through with a twenty at Christmas.

Q. I'm expecting my first child next month and my husband seems more than a bit reluctant about it. He was a lot less reluctant eight months ago, of course. How can I tell what kind of a father a man will be?

A. That's easy. All men turn out to be the same kind of father. That is, reluctant. But don't worry. Most men love their children with a devotion so fierce that it rivals their love for *Hogan's Heroes* reruns. It's just that they are totally bewildered when it comes to care and maintenance. As a friend of mine, and new father, once said to me, "If God had meant for a man to get up for the four o'clock feeding, he would have given us tits." He was killed shortly thereafter, the unfortunate victim of a tragic accident involving his wife and a flying five-pound can of "Similac."

Men are awed by newborns. They are amazed that a ten-pound child can turn four ounces of strained squash into eighteen pounds of poop in a matter of minutes. They are frightened motionless by the child who can shriek at decibel levels normally attained only by military aircraft. Except for purchasing the occasional box of disposable diapers, men are innocent bystanders in the early stages of child rearing.

It is only as the child gets a little older, say early teens, that a Dad swings into action in his only truly comfortable role. That is, the enforcer. And he will then do to his child all the horrible things that his father did to him, the punishments that he hated, the yelling and screaming he swore he would never do. Men do this because, "Hell, it was good enough for me, it's good enough for my kid."

Male logic at its most irrefutable.

Section Seven

ASTROLOGICAL SIGNS OF MEN

What The Stars Say

ARIES
The Ram
March 21st through April 20th

Aries is the sign of the Ram and the Aries man is easily identifiable by his tendency to butt his head against large, immovable objects. Some even have hooves. Aries men are talkative, self-involved sorts who can have just as much fun on a date with as without you. As a matter of fact, so involved are they in their tales of business acquisitions and sports trivia, they may not even notice when you dash to the ladies' room and never return.

The Aries man is impulsive, quick to anger and can make love for minutes at a time, or longer if you leave the television on. It's not that the Ram has a short attention span, it's just that he usually has a couple hundred riding on a meaningless sporting event somewhere in the world and needs to stay on top of things. Which is his favorite position.

Always generous to a fault, the Aries man is a big tipper and often calls waitresses "Honey" or "Sugar" or "Mambo Jugs."

TAURUS
The Bull
April 21st through May 21st

It is often said that the whole male population can be found under the bull. Er, I mean, the *sign* of the Bull. Taurus men are brave and at the same time stupid. Like their namesake, they enjoy impaling small Spaniards and urinating in open fields.

The Taurean is a man of few words and not many more syllables. With a usable vocabulary of about 150 words, men born in the sign of the Bull are down-to-earth sorts, homebodies who rarely make a move without a portable TV in hand.

The Taurus male is a man's man who is content with the simple things in life, like Mom, apple pie, and the girl next door, especially if she has really big breasts.

Tranquility and peace are the keys to a happy life for a Taurus man and he is content to spend his time sunk deep into his recliner in front of the tube with a six pack. But don't get the Bull angry! Try to switch from "The Pro Bowler's Tour" to some stupid public TV show while he's napping and you'll run the risk of igniting his horrible Taurus temper. He may even get out of his chair for a minute or two to wrestle the remote control away from you.

GEMINI
The Twins
May 22nd through June 21st

The man born under the sign of the Twins is two-faced, no question about that. But how does this make him different from other men? Men who say they are dating *you* exclusively but then refuse to play the messages on their answering machine in your presence because they might be *personal*? Well, it doesn't, actually. All men are two-faced, lying scum where dating is involved. The Gemini man, however, is in a class all by himself.

A Gemini man is quick to change his mind, his opinions and his attitudes, but unfortunately not so quick to change his underclothes. He has the attention span of a six week-old Cocker Spaniel and hygeine habits to match. Keep the remote control channel changer away from this man! The Gemini man can't stand not having control. As he drives he will twirl the radio dial incessantly in a search for the perfect song, skipping back and forth until you want to break his fingers. Try to do this at a stoplight where it won't cause an accident.

CANCER
The Crab
June 22nd through July 23rd

The Cancerian is a moody, cranky man who's likely to scream at anyone who leaves the top off the toothpaste tube or puts an empty jar back in the refrigerator. Of course, you'd be moody and cranky too if your Sun sign was named after pubic lice. A Cancer man is a child of the moon and you'll often find him alone on his roof, gazing through a high-powered telescope at the magnificent lunar landscape. And at the bedroom window of his neighbor's 17-year-old daughter.

Cancer is a thrifty sign and the Crab dude's idea of a big night on the town is miniature golf and a couple of Big Macs. For this he'll expect to be treated like a king, especially if he wins a free game by getting a hole-in-one on the last hole.

A Cancer man loves to be in the fashion vanguard. No slave to current trends and good taste, the Crab goes his own way. An orange tie with embroidered hula girls and ukeleles coupled with a Hawaiian shirt (100% Rayon) and bell-bottomed jeans and he's dressed to kill. And when he comes to your best friend's wedding that way you may want to. Kill him, that is.

LEO

The Lion
July 24th through August 23rd

The Leo man is generally a gregarious, whimsical sort who enjoys looking up the definitions of vulgar words in unabridged dictionaries. Leos are proud, independent men who love to be their own boss. They especially enjoy drinking coffee out of cups with wacky sayings on them like "You don't have to be crazy to work here but it helps!"

Leo men love to be the center of attention and never pass up the chance to be drunk and obnoxious in public. They often wear colorful, unusual underwear and aren't bashful about showing it off.

Lions are subject to frequent colds and other illnesses and when sick will whine a lot and keep you running for hot tea with lemon, saltine crackers and Archie comic books. If you balk at performing these tasks, the proud Leo will sulk and pout and call his mother on the phone to report hourly on his temperature and the texture of his stool.

If you're a career gal, Leo is not the man for you. He prefers his wife/girlfriend/spousal equivalent to be home, nearby where he can slap her on the rump now and again and say with a smug grin "My wife/girlfriend/spousal equivalent! I think I'll keep her!"

VIRGO
The Virgin
August 24th
through September 23rd

Yes, Virgo is the sign of the Virgin. But don't let that fool you! Most Virgo men have plenty of hot, kinky sex. However, they're usually alone when they have it. You see, Virgos are loners by nature and they like to take matters into their own hands. When married, the Virgo man may even forget he has a mate. This can be disconcerting when, after three years of marriage, your Virgo man asks you at the breakfast table who you are and what the hell you're doing with his raisin toast.

The Virgo man is an incessantly tidy creature. This Felix Unger of the Zodiac will be put out in the extreme should you forget to use a coaster, or if you put the just washed glasses in the cupboard without turning them upside down to dry. He'll never actually *say* anything about these horrible habits of yours, though. He'll just follow you from room to room with a box of moist towelettes and a can of Lemon Pledge, wiping and spraying and sighing a martyr's sigh. Not surprisingly, Virgo males are victims in more domestic murders than any other star sign.

LIBRA

The Scales
September 24th
through October 23rd

The Libra man has a finely tuned sense of justice, of balance, of what's right and what's wrong. He will gladly take out the garbage in exchange for your doing the dishes, the laundry, the floors, the bathrooms and the beds.

Romantic *and* frugal, your Libra lover will *never* smother you with a dozen red roses and a box of candy. His feeling is that such displays are tacky and tasteless. Instead he'll bring his ladylove a single perfect rose because, as a Libra friend once confided, "What the hell. She thinks it's a suave move and I save thirty bucks." The Libra man also pronounces "suave" as though it were spelled "swave."

Many a man's physical appearance reflects his Zodiacal sign (a Leo's mane of hair, and a Taurus' rather dopey, bovine expression) and Libra men are no exception. They often suffer from scaly, dry skin and consume 30% of the dandruff shampoo and eczema lotion in the U.S.

SCORPIO
The Scorpion
October 24th through November 22nd

Scorpio is the sign of a passionate and fiery temperament, the sign of heroes and warriors. The Scorpio man is likely to be a leader and decision maker and wear his hat at a jaunty angle.

No job is too big or intimidating for the powerful Scorp. Never content to simply mow the lawn and empty the trash, the Scorpio man will bend over backwards to uproot trees and destroy entire plumbing systems in wild fits of helpfulness.

Scorpio is the ruler of the sex organs and as such spends an inordinate amount of time scratching himself as though his shorts were too tight. He is also very susceptible to injury in that area which is why so many Scorpios sing tenor.

While the November man often appears cool and collected on the outside, he can be a seething cauldron on the inside. Especially since his favorite foods are jalapenos and banana daiquiris. Yes, the weak and timid are advised to stay away from the Scorpion, whose gas can kill house pets at twenty paces.

SAGITTARIUS
The Archer
November 23rd
through December 21st

Sagittarian men are usually animal lovers and often have criminal records because of it. They are daredevils and risk takers who go in for dangerous sports like cliff diving and race car driving. Not actually doing those things, you understand, but they watch them on TV a lot. They're not stupid, you know.

Sagittarians have lots of terrific qualities. They're loyal, brave, thrifty, clean and reverent. And they can make a campfire by rubbing two sticks together. These things are often foolishly overlooked by women in search of a man with money, brains and looks. Well, Sagittarian men get along quite well without any of these things, I can assure you!

The Sagittarius man is a flirt and a romantic and loves to refer to woman as "gals." He comes on to every waitress and receptionist he meets because it comes so naturally to him that he just can't help himself. And besides, he figures it never hurts to get a little on the side.

CAPRICORN
The Goat
December 22nd
through January 20th

Capricorn is the slow and steady sign of the Zodiac. You'll have to look very closely and learn quite a bit about your Capricorn man's habits before you'll be able to tell if he's awake or asleep. This is an ambitious sign and the industrious Capricorn will strive constantly to improve himself, taking night classes in pottery making, yodeling, anything to get ahead.

Capricorn men love beautiful poems, especially that one that goes..."There once was a girl from Nantucket..." This is a practical man who will wear the same pair of sneakers for years, until the original color is unrecognizable and you have to peel them off his feet with a crow bar while he's asleep. Luckily, that usually turns out to be a good portion of the day. Don't forget to wear rubber gloves!

Capricorn men are notorious babblers who will corner you at a party and drill a hole in you with their talk about cars, politics or business. They often get that weird white spittle at the corners of their mouths, too, the kind that gets all stringy and stretches from lip to lip while they talk so that you can't look at anything else and you think you might barf if they don't shut up.

AQUARIUS
The Water Bearer
January 21st through February 19th

I'm not exactly sure what a Water Bearer is but Aquarian men do seem to have to stop at gas stations a lot on long car trips.

Aquarians are dreamers and optimists. They always see their glass of beer as being half full, not half empty. Especially if there's another cold six pack in the fridge.

Aquarians have little regard for authority and flagrantly flout it at every opportunity. They think nothing of tearing the tags off their pillows and recklessly use Q-Tips *inside* their ear canals. This sort of behavior can be very exciting for Aquarian men who are ruled by the planet Uranus and if you think I'm going to use that as an excuse to make some crude, low brow joke about hemorrhoids or constipation or saying something like, "His rising sign is in Uranus," you can just forget about it.

PISCES
The Fish
February 20th through March 20th

Pisces men are born practical jokers who love to liven up the office by shaking an important client's hand with a joy buzzer on or slipping a whoopee cushion on to the bosses' chair. Not surprisingly, men born under the sign of the Fish are frequently unemployed. Despite this, Pisces are unflaggingly generous when it comes to their money. They love to buy rounds of cocktails for complete strangers in bars and will do so with the slightest provocation. Even if it means the landlord has to wait a few weeks for the rent.

Men born under the sign of the Fish are dreamers. Their idea of planning for the future is checking the television movie guide two days in advance. Pisces is the sign of musicians, artists, writers and all sorts of other occupations men take up in order to avoid getting a real job. Many Pisces men are on a first name basis with the whole gang down at the unemployment office, and are always invited to their Christmas parties.

Still, for all his faults, the Pisces man is a romantic one. Shiftlessness, unpredictability, thoughtlessness and inability to commit, communicate or hold a job, are all traits of Pisces men. I guess that's why they get all the chicks.

Section Eight

MALESPEAK: A TEST
The Secret Language of Men

The following multiple choice questions are designed to test your ability to understand just what in the hell it is that men are talking about half the time. It may not be as scientific or reliable as those dopey tests you find in women's magazines about "How Well You Know Your Lover's Bodily Functions" or "Are You A Match Made in Hell?" but heck, I gave it my best shot.

1. He drops you off on your doorstep after a date, kisses you in a friendly way and says "I'll call you." This really means:

    A. "I'll call you as soon as I get home because I am completely entranced by you."

    B. "I'll call you if I can squeeze it into my schedule."

    C. "I'll call you if my steady girlfriend starts giving me a hard time again."

    D. "I'll never call you."

    E. All of the above.

2. He is camped in front of the tube glued to some brutal and meaningless sporting event. The garbage bag under the sink is threatening to take over the entire kitchen. You ask him to take it out. He says, "In a minute, Honey." This really means:

    A. "At half-time."

    B. "When the game's over."

    C. "When this game, the next game and the 'Sports Wrap Up' shows are over."

D. "If I procrastinate long enough I bet you'll get sick of waiting and take it out yourself."

E. All of the above.

3. He is sitting at the dinner table in front of a burger and a large order of fries. You are upstairs dressing for an important event that you are attending solo. He hollers from his chair "Honey! Where's the ketchup?" This really means:

A. "You forgot to ask for extra ketchup again, didn't you?"

B. "Get me the ketchup."

C. "I can't believe you're going out without me tonight and I'm really pissed off about it.

D. All of the above.

4. You attend a large family gathering at which he meets your younger sister for the first time. On the ride home he says, "Boy, how come you didn't tell me Becky was such a knockout?" This really means:

A. "Boy, you're getting fat, aren't you?"

B. "Now I know where all the looks in your family went."

C. "I wonder if she'd ever go out with me if I dumped you."

D. All of the above.

5. You have been dating for a good long while. He looks deep into your eyes and says "I think it's time we moved in together." This really means:

    A. "My lease is up next month, and the landlord wants to raise my rent."

    B. "If you're gonna be here this often you might as well pay for it."

    C. "Your TV is a lot bigger than mine is, and you get cable, too."

    D. All of the above.

6. You are having a quiet dinner at home. Talk turns toward your past. He asks "What was your old boyfriend like?" This really means:

    A. "Was he better looking than me?"

    B. "Did he make more money than me?"

    C. "Was he better in bed than me?"

    D. "How big was his dick?"

    E. All of the above.

7. You have just made love. You lie peacefully in his arms. Perhaps you smoke a cigarette. He asks "Was it good for you?" This really means:

    A. "Did you come?"

    B. "Am I the best lover you've ever had?"

    C. "You're not gonna want to do it again are you? 'I'm beat."

    D. "You weren't faking it, were you?"

    E. All of the above.

8. He asks "Will you marry me?" This really means:

    A. "Will you pick up my dirty socks for the rest of my life?"

    B. "Will you still love me when I'm old and fat and bald?"

    C. "Will you make sandwiches for the boys on poker night?"

    D. "Will you change your name to mine even though it means changing all your credit cards and your driver's license and even though your name is Smith and mine is Glyzxkowskokzowicz?"

    E. All of the above.

ANSWERS:

As all seasoned test takers know, when in doubt choose "All of the above." Which is the correct answer for all of the above.

TEN THINGS MEN ARE ACTUALLY GOOD FOR

1. Can deftly handle all VCR remote control options.

2. Can explain pro hockey's "offsides" rules.

3. Will squash ugly, hairy spiders.

4. Can light the barbecue on the first try every time.

5. Knows where to get "Neats Foot Oil" and how to properly oil and break in your new softball glove.

6. Can assemble and connect stereo components.

7. Knows where to rent and how to operate heavy duty machinery like "snakes", "winches" and "post-hole diggers."

8. They change flat tires.

9. Knows where to get really good illegal 4th of July fireworks.

10. About once every two years, actually notices you got all dressed up for him.

About the author:

Tom Carey is a writer/cartoonist/philosopher who lives in Chicago and dispenses advice about Love, Life and Relationships to his friends who pay attention to him not one little bit. He is single, 31 years old, has no known allergies, flosses regularly and his most fervent ambition is to appear in *Cosmopolitan* as the "Bachelor of the Month."

He is a Scorpio.